AUTHOR

Gabriele Malavoglia was born in Milan in 1989. After completing his high school studies, he moved to Spain to pursue his university studies, remaining on Iberian soil after graduation. Passionate since childhood about Italian and Spanish Military History, he is a self-taught scholar and is taking his first steps in the field of editorialism. He lives in Zaragoza and works as a logistics consultant for some local companies.

PUBLISHING'S NOTES

None of unpublished images or text of our book may be reproduced in any format without the expressed written permission of Luca Cristini Editore (already Soldiershop.com) when not indicate as marked with license creative commons 3.0 or 4.0. Luca Cristini Editore has made every reasonable effort to locate, contact and acknowledge rights holders and to correctly apply terms and conditions to Content.

Every effort has been made to trace the copyright of all the photographs. If there are unintentional omissions, please contact the publisher in writing at: info@soldiershop.com, who will correct all subsequent editions.

Our trademark: Luca Cristini Editore©, and the names of our series & brand: Soldiershop, Witness to war, Museum book, Bookmoon, Soldiers&Weapons, Battlefield, War in colour, Historical Biographies, Darwin's view, Fabula, Altrastoria, Italia Storica Ebook, Witness To History, Soldiers, Weapons & Uniforms, Storia etc. are herein © by Luca Cristini Editore.

LICENSES COMMONS

This book may utilize part of material marked with license creative commons 3.0 or 4.0 (CC BY 4.0), (CC BY-ND 4.0), (CC BY-SA 4.0) or (CC0 1.0). We give appropriate attribution credit and indicate if change were made in the acknowledgments field. Our WTW books series utilize only fonts licensed under the SIL Open Font License or other free use license.

For a complete list of Soldiershop titles please contact Luca Cristini Editore on our website: www.soldiershop.com or www.cristinieditore.com. E-mail: info@soldiershop.com

Title: **TANKS OF THE SPANISH CIVIL WAR - VOL. 3** Code.: **WTW-053 EN** by Gabriele Malavoglia
ISBN code: 9791255890584 First edition January 2024
Text: English; layout: 177,8 x 254mm Cover & Art Design: Luca S. Cristini

WITNESS TO WAR (SOLDIERSHOP) is a trademark of Luca Cristini Editore, via Orio 33D - 24050 Zanica (BG) ITALY.

WITNESS TO WAR

TANKS OF THE SPANISH CIVIL WAR VOL. 3

PROTOTYPES AND TIZNAOS

PHOTOS & IMAGES FROM WORLD WARTIME ARCHIVES

GABRIELE MALAVOGLIA

BOOKS TO COLLECT

CONTENTS

Introduction..5

Tiznaos..7

    Constructora Field in Barcelona..15

    Ebro armoured trucks..15

    Mercier II armoured car...35

    Torras armoured trucks...35

    Girona armoured trucks..36

    Ferrol armoured trucks...36

    Colouring of the "tiznaos"..39

Spanish-made prototypes..75

    Carro Ligero Trubia Serie A Modelo 1926...75

    Carro de Combate Ligero Para Infantería Modelo 1936....................................79

    "Trubia – Naval" tank..79

    Carro de Combate de Infantería Tipo 1937...83

    Barbastro tank...84

    IGC Sadurní de Noya tank..85

    Landesa tank...88

    Verdeja tank..90

    UNL Goliath armoured truck..95

    Oteyza model 1935 armoured truck...95

Acknowledgements..96

Bibliography...97

INTRODUCTION

After having dealt in previous volumes with fundamental topics such as the organisation and history of Republican and Nationalist armoured units (Volume 1) and the different armoured vehicles used in the Spanish Civil War, we will address in these pages two more focal topics related to the armoured vehicles fielded in Spain, during what was the first real 'armoured' war in history.
First and foremost, we will deal with the analysis of those absolutely 'typical' objects of the conflict, the armoured trucks, the so-called 'Tiznaos', the true icon of the Iberian conflict. The armoured trucks were born as an artisanal and, dare I say it, spontaneous response to the endless hunger for armoured vehicles to be used in the maelstrom of the Civil War and still represent a characteristic feature in the collective imagination.
Another interesting (and misunderstood) aspect is the remarkable conception and production of tank prototypes, generated by the felt need to achieve the industrial production of a 'national' tank, conceived, born and built in Spain, with which to arm the armoured units, which had by then proved necessary and unavoidable in the context of modern warfare.

▲ The Tiznaos were civil vehicles converted into armoured vehicles by local industries and metalworkers. In the photo, a group of workers in a workshop set up by the NTC intent on producing an armoured truck.

▲ Detail of the delicate phase of welding the plates that served as armour protection on the vehicle in the previous photograph.

▼ One of the many models of homemade armoured vehicles that were manufactured during the Spanish Civil War, photographed in Barcelona in 1936. On the armour can be read the initials of the anarchist movements CNT - Confederacion Nacional de Trabajo and FAI - Federaciòn Anarquista Ibérica.

TIZNAOS

The 'tiznaos' were the most distinctive military vehicles of the Spanish Civil War and deserve a specific and as in-depth analysis as possible, despite the scarcity of information available.

As seen in previous volumes, when the Civil War broke out in Spain in 1936, both sides in the conflict were suffering from a shortage of military means[1] and were in a situation of dependence on foreign powers, which supplied them with armaments, materials and means. Both the Republicans (mainly) and the Nationalists (to a lesser extent) resorted to ingenuity to create improvised armoured vehicles to make up for the lack of armoured vehicles and tanks. The tactics of warfare widespread in Europe in the 1930s involved a massive use of infantry, still employed as a static force in the trenches, although the first theories were spreading that advocated a more fluid use of soldiers, with the support of armoured vehicles, which in Spain were numerically scarce and qualitatively obsolete, namely the Schneider M16 CA1, Renault FT17 and nationally produced armoured cars (*see volume 2 of this series*).

The first units to resort to the use of these circumstantial armoured vehicles were the paramilitary formations, as the tanks and armoured cars supplied by foreign countries were intended for the regular military units, for use in the front line, while the various paramilitary formations mostly acted in the second line and in urban environments, although there was no lack of participation in direct warfare actions. Until the arrival of tanks supplied by the Soviet Union, the 'tiznaos' remained practically the only armoured component of the Republican Armed Forces.

In fact, Spain was not new to the use of armoured trucks. In 1914, the Spanish Army had purchased 24 armoured trucks from the French Schneider - Creusot, built on PB2 buses, normally used in Parisian public transport. Later, in 1922, a dozen (the exact number is not known) armoured troop transport vehicles were built on the Latil truck chassis in the Iberian Peninsula; these vehicles were used as artillery tractors for medium-calibre pieces, at the same time transporting piece servants and ammunition. Both Schneider and Latil vehicles were used to transport troops during the war in Morocco, only to be used again as artillery tractors by the 19th Artillery Regiment at the end of the conflict.

During the early stages of the Civil War, the Republican trade union organisations took to the streets of the cities, with the aim of suppressing any possible action by the Nationalists, by patrolling the town centres on board requisitioned commercial trucks. The sad experience of the first few days taught them that, in order to defend themselves against the action of any snipers, these trucks had to be equipped in some way with protection, and so materials such as sheet metal, wooden planks, mattresses, sandbags and anything else that could offer shelter from enemy fire were employed. Soon these fallback solutions saw an evolution and the trucks received better designed and better made armour, although a widespread level of standardisation could never be achieved.

In the more industrialised areas controlled by the Republicans, such as Catalonia, Levante and the Basque Country, a sort of 'arms race' began, armouring as many vehicles as possible with makeshift means to send to the front. Practically anyone who had access to a machine shop and could find one or more vehicles on wheels (any organised group of workers, trade unions, anarchists or simple political circles) made extravagant and improbable armoured vehicles.

These armoured trucks took on the name 'tiznao', referring to the dark colour of the welded sheet metal, a colour that the vehicles had due to the craftsmanship process followed in the workshops

---

1 The Spanish war industry was rather backward in development and had in fact never undertaken any serious studies on the construction of national tanks.

and that gave them a dirty and rusty appearance, although they were sometimes painted in a military or camouflage colour. According to other sources, however, the name was derived from the fact that the vehicles were often covered in grease, since, it was believed, this would make it easier to repel enemy bullets, giving the vehicles a blackish appearance: this earned the improvised trucks the nickname 'tiznao', from the adjective 'tiznado', meaning sooty.

The materials used to armour these vehicles were metal plates of different qualities and heterogeneous thicknesses and, in some extreme cases, mattresses tied with ropes to the sides of the trucks were also used, as had been done in the first weeks of the conflict. The lack of design and specific technical preparation of the manufacturers in the field of armoured vehicles led at times to the erroneous conviction that very thick and robust armour plating would offer greater defence, not taking into account that this made many of these vehicles too heavy, thus limiting their manoeuvring capacity and considerably restricting their speed, effectively preventing their use on rough terrain. The purpose of the armour plating was to protect the driver, the crew, the riflemen carried in the body, but also the tyres, the transmission components and the engine. Often, however, due to the use of scrap material for the armour, the structure of the 'tiznaos' was shoddy and they were often quickly disposed of in combat. Only those with a better conception and design, such as those built in Barcelona, managed to have a longer operational life and, in some cases, reach the end of the Spanish War practically intact.

For the construction of these improvised vehicles, the chassis of commercial vehicles (MAN, Mercedes, Chevrolet, Ford, Renault...) were generally used, as they were only equipped with two-wheel drive, which made them unsuitable for off-road routes. Although born from many different designs, even in distant locations, the 'tiznaos' all shared the same basic construction principle: an armoured superstructure built on top of a truck chassis, with additional protection at the front, doors to enter and exit the vehicle at the rear or sides, and loopholes along the vehicle, which allowed the occupants to fire small arms. In fact, therefore, the general layout closely followed that of the Schneider trucks purchased in 1914, which were probably taken as a model by the manufacturers.

Their value in combat was rather limited, but their presence served to boost the morale of the Republican troops. The weight of the armour, which was excessive for the frames used, and the overstressing to which the suspensions were subjected prevented their use off-road, but their disproportionate size made them veritable monsters of metal, capable of instilling psychological terror in their adversaries. A widespread tactic of employment among the Republicans was deployed when particular strategic locations were threatened by the Nationalists. Long columns of trucks and 'tiznaos', carrying at least a dozen men each, were deployed along the roads at the threatened positions. Often, when operating in this manner, large progressive numbers in white, black or red were painted on the 'tiznaos' to better identify the vehicles.

Cars, lorries, buses, pick-ups and even trains and agricultural and construction machinery were armoured; consequently, due to the great variety of vehicles used as the basis for the 'tiznaos' and the skill and 'taste' of the mechanics who were in charge of armour plating, there were practically no two vehicles that were identical, which makes the meticulous treatment and cataloguing of them practically impossible. To make classification even more difficult, one must add the fact that there is practically no factory documentation relating to the 'tiznaos'[2] . A macro-subdivision between manufactured means can be made by distinguishing improvised means from factory-made conversions. Among the improvised vehicles can be considered those fielded during the early stages of the Spanish Civil War, characterised, as we have seen above, by armoured vehicles assembled using any available material, without following even the slightest planning, often by workshops not equipped

---

[2] In his book 'Carros De Combats Y Véhiculas Blindados de la Guerra 1936-1939', published by Borras in 1980, P.C. Albert identifies 14 different models, which adopted forms as diverse as they were varied, but in reality, as can be seen in the photographic section of this book, an impressive number of different and unique models of tiznaos were made.

to build armoured vehicles. The second category, that of conversions, includes armoured vehicles made in workshops that we can define as 'specialised' (or explicitly reconverted for war production), following a production process more similar to an 'industrial' concept, therefore based, first and foremost, on the design of the vehicle.

The 'tiznaos' proliferated particularly in the Republican faction, as the economic means at their disposal were significantly less, as were the supplies of armoured vehicles from foreign countries[3] . Nevertheless, when one of these improvised armoured vehicles was captured by the Nationalists, it was often immediately redeployed and sent back to the battlefield. The Nationalists, when they began to receive substantial supplies of tanks from Italy and Germany, soon learnt to put the 'tiznaos' out of action through the unscrupulous use of artillery or with mined air attacks, as they no longer had the urgency to recover these improvised armoured vehicles from the enemy.

Although they were built substantially throughout the territory in Republican hands, the production of 'tiznaos' was concentrated more significantly, for different reasons, in a few specific areas. In particular, cut off from the rest of the Republic, the industrial north was where most of these vehicles were built: the factories of the SECN, Sestao and Trubia already had experience in the construction of military vehicles and 'mass' production (as far as one can speak of 'mass' production for this type of vehicle) began around December 1936. In an attempt to counterbalance the advances of the Ejército de África, the small industrial centres of Andalusia and Extremadura produced some rudimentary 'tiznaos' of questionable value, as did the industrial apparatuses linked to the mines of Riotinto (Huelva) and the factories of Linares, which fought the advance of the Ejército de África and supported the war effort on the Cordoba front. In Extremadura, the 'tiznaos' built in Don Benito and some other towns and villages in the region were unable to make any effective contribution to the resistance against the Francoists' advance. The other most industrialised region in the territory controlled by the Republicans was Catalonia: official documents show that at least 159 'tiznaos' were built between July 1936 and August 1937 and at least 33 more in the following period. The main factories involved in the construction of these vehicles were Comité Metalúrgico Villafranca (1 example), Constructora Field (13 examples), Casa Girona (21 examples), Hispano-Suiza (38 examples), Maquinista Terrestre y Marítima (also known as MTM - 22 examples), Sindicato Metalúrgico de Badalona (4 examples), Casa Torras (43 examples) and Casa Vulcano (17 examples). The region of Valencia and Murcia was also prolific in the construction of 'tiznaos', most of which were produced by the Unión Naval de Levante (UNL). Let's look at some of them in detail.

---

[3] Behind the supply of armoured vehicles to the factions involved in the Spanish Civil War, in addition to the obvious support for the cause that supported their political ideals, one can also see an interest in field-testing their armoured vehicles and armoured cars in a real conflict. After the beginnings of the armoured weapon during the Great War and until then, in fact, technical-constructive developments and doctrines of armoured vehicle engagement had only been able to develop on paper; the only exception was the Abyssinian campaign for Italy, which was in any case facing an enemy that was completely devoid of tanks. The War in Spain, therefore, represented an opportunity too good to miss for the Powers of the day.

▲ A truck, probably Chevrolet, converted into an armoured car; the slogan on the bonnet cover reads 'Frente Poular - Don Benito'.

▼ Photograph taken in Bilbado of a civilian truck, used by a wine merchant, transformed into an armoured vehicle: the armour plating was completely covered with Republican slogans.

▲ Brave Republican volunteers pose aboard a Tiznao titled 'To the memory of the martyrs of liberty', as stated on the front armouring. The vehicle is painted entirely in grey.

▲ This old armoured truck received the battle name 'Ghost'; we know that it was the second vehicle to receive this nickname and that it was employed by the Ejército Popular de Asturias.

▼ The 'tiznao' 'Ghost No. 12' of the People's Army of Asturias, similar to the vehicle in the previous photograph.

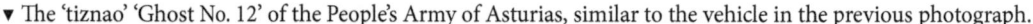

▲ Greek anarchists, fighters in the ranks of the CNT, in front of a Tiznao (on the sides the inscription 'Hermanos no tirar', 'Soldiers don't shoot') appearing on numerous republican armoured trucks, to avoid falling victim to friendly fire).

▼ The same 'tiznao' as in the previous photograph. The picture also shows the inscriptions on other parts of the vehicle 'Viva la Republica' and the number 3, probably traced with white paint.

▲ Entrance of the so-called 'Durruti Column' in Alcalá Street in Madrid in November 1936. Three different Tiznaos open the column.

▼ Two Tiznaos, one of them transported in a civilian truck, prepare to leave for the front, inside the Bakunin barracks in Barcelona, 1936. The 'tiznao' on the left is the 'Girona 3', while the one on the truck is the 'Girona 4'.

CONSTRUCTORA FIELD IN BARCELONA

Among these manufacturers, the production of Constructora Field del Poble Nou in Barcelona, which produced boilers in peacetime, was very interesting. For this reason, the vessels of this factory had a peculiar shape that made them resemble an enormous boiler, cut lengthwise in half, formed from hot-bent steel plates. The different components (probably four large main plates, complemented by a series of smaller secondary elements) were then welded together to give shape to the armour, which thus took on a unique shape, adapted to the chassis of the truck on which they were working. It is probable that part of the structure, which perhaps rested on a wooden frame, was held together by small rivets. Access to the vehicle was from the rear, even for the driver, as there were no side doors. All these 'tiznaos' were equipped with large ventilation tubes, similar to the wind-sleeves of ships, mounted on the front of the vehicle; the wheels were protected by movable shields, which could be lifted to service the tyres, while the lower part of the vehicles was protected by armoured 'skirts' or chains. The rounded shape made the vehicles produced in Barcelona resemble 'monsters' and particularly ballistically resistant to small arms fire.

Constructora Field's vehicles were also known, unofficially, as 'Barcelona' or 'Truck Blindado 4×2 No.8'. About ten examples were made, characterised by this aerodynamic design from the boiler plates and the iconic lettering on the front of the vehicle.

The prototype of the Constructora Fields was completed on 29 August 1936 and, on the same day, was presented to the press and, the following day, was also presented to the people of Barcelona, with the FAI inscription, in the presence of the President of Catalonia Lluís Companys. The main differences between the prototype and the 'series' vehicles, as far as it makes sense to speak of series production for the 'tiznaos' are the absence of the turret, which appeared from Model 'No. 2' onwards, and the orientation of the air intakes, which were rearward-facing in the prototype.

The Constructora Fields had a number of critical issues. One major problem was the difficulty in accessing the engine, as there was only a small hatch at the front, which did not allow for major maintenance. It cannot be ruled out that the entire upper shield of the engine could be lifted, but this is only a hypothesis. Another critical issue was the overheating of the propulsion apparatus, which was put under strain by the weight of the armour, aggravated in some examples by the presence of the turret, and not sufficiently ventilated by the small grilles on the vehicles, which made the time needed to cool the engine, even when stationary, extremely long. Furthermore, like most of the other 'tiznaos', due to their high ground pressure, the Constructora Fields could not be used for off-road travel.

Among Constructora Fields' armoured vehicles, we can also count some examples made according to a completely different construction scheme, i.e. with convex armour and turrets with a different shape to the other vehicles of the Barcelona-based company. On the front of these curious vehicles, in fact, appears the inscription 'CONSTRUCTORA FIELD BARCELONA', which traces them back to the same metal industry. Some sources claim that this is a late production, others that these vehicles are referable to Model 'N°4'.

EBRO ARMOURED TRUCKS

The armoured trucks named 'Ebro' were produced by several companies in Zaragoza, Aragon, where the industry dedicated to the production of agricultural and railway mechanical components flourished, during the first months of the Civil War; they were very well designed, although they had practically no off-road capability and were characterised by reduced armouring, suitable only for protection from small arms fire. All the 'tiznao' produced in the Aragonese capital were named

▲ Tiznaos of the Nationalists in San Sebastián. The deck on the left was commonly referred to as the 'Pamplona' and the movement of the wheel guards is peculiar, which can be clearly seen in the photograph. The driver had a small slit at the front for a view of the road, while he had no possibility of seeing to the side: this made driving this 'tiznao' particularly difficult. The number 3 in black painted on the side served to indicate the position of the vehicle within the column of vehicles to which it belonged. The armoured truck on the right, on the other hand, was originally Republican and had been captured in Navarre and re-used by the Francoists.

▼ Republican Tiznao in front of the Grand Casino of San Sebastián (now the city's City Hall) in 1936. The front plate was specially shaped to allow the projection of the lighthouse beam; the armour structure appears to be supported by a set of metal rods.

▲ Another armoured truck near the Casino in San Sebastián.

▼ Gudari (Basque militiamen supporting the Republican cause) posing in front of an 'Echeverría' armoured truck on the Biscay front.

▲ Armoured truck built by the Republican militia to defend against the uprising in San Sebastián.

▼ An old Nash-Quad M21 truck, armoured for the Rif war, recovered and transferred to San Sebastián, on the Biscay front, at the outbreak of the Civil War by the Loyola rebels (Filmoteca Española).

▲ On this Tiznao stands the inscription 'Captured from the enemy in the sector of Marquina': this is a town in the north of Spain, about fifty kilometres from Bilbao, famous for the extraction of black marble.

▼ An armoured truck used by anarchists from the first days in Barcelona, with the painted initials of the CNT, FAI, POUM and UHP.

▲ Workshop of the Constructora Naval de Sestao, where four republican Renault FT17 tanks, two 'tiznaos' and an armoured tractor are being serviced.

▼ Armoured truck used in the early war periods; it was believed that the very sloping shape of the casemate, found on other 'tiznaos', offered higher protection to the occupants of the vehicle.

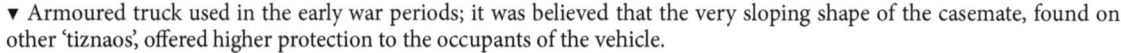

▲ Armoured vehicle of the CNT - FAI, belonging to the Durruti Column. This was a non-regular military formation, formed mostly of anarchists and communists, commanded by the anarchist trade unionist leader Buenaventura Durruti, who died in the first months of the war, from whom it took its name. With 3,000 men, the Column was first deployed on the front in Aragon and then in Madrid.

▼ The same armoured truck as the Durruti Column on the Aragon front, made by the 'Maquinista Terrestre y Maritima' in Barcelona.

▲ Another armoured truck of the Durruti Column, built by Talleres Serra, framed in the '19 de Julio' regiment, photographed on the Aragon front.

▲ Armoured vehicle named 'Casimiro Velasco' of the Ejército Popular de Asturias, destroyed in Oviedo in October 1936.

▲ A 'tiznao' almost identical to the previous one, also photographed in the Oviedo circle.

▲ Vehicles like this, on a Bedford truck chassis, were used in the failed landings in Majorca at the beginning of the Civil War.

▼ An image taken in Majorca on 6 September 1936 of the armoured vehicles that participated with the so-called 'Bayo Column' in the failed attempt to invade the island.

▲ A 'tiznao' captured at the Bayo Column, during the battle for Majorca.

▼ A group of Banyalbufarin phalangists rushed to defend Son Servera during the landing of Republican troops in Portocristo.

▲ Truck seized from the Republicans in Crémenes in 1936; the armour plating is riddled with bullets, demonstrating the poor protection offered by this type of artisanal vehicle (Heraclito Archive).

▼ Ebro front: Republican 'tiznaos' knocked out by enemy fire and captured by Nationalists.

▲ Armoured tracked tractor of the CNT-FAI in Barcelona in October 1936. The vehicle was lost at an unspecified date and place on the Aragon front.

▼ Another armoured tractor, built on the same mechanics as the previous one but with a different armour design, captured by the Nationalists. On the sides of the vehicle were inscriptions praising the Soviet Union.

▲ A Republican armoured vehicle captured by the Nationalists in Oviedo; the starting vehicle appears to be an old MAN truck.

▼ The armour plating of this Asturian 'tiznao' was completely covered in grease, because it was thought that this arrangement made the vehicle more resistant to gunfire. The photo was taken in Gijón in July 1936.

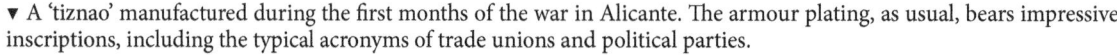

▲ Interesting about this 'tiznao' captured by the Nationalists at Andoain is the addition of a cannon to the rear of the vehicle.

▼ A 'tiznao' manufactured during the first months of the war in Alicante. The armour plating, as usual, bears impressive inscriptions, including the typical acronyms of trade unions and political parties.

▲ Another homemade armoured truck: the photo was undoubtedly taken in the early days of the conflict, as the militiamen on board appear all smiles, as if they were going on a pleasure trip, not yet aware of the horror they will have to face. The vehicle is entirely covered with slogans praising Communism.

▼ The 'tiznaos' were often employed to escort mobile columns, sent to areas of greatest danger or where fiercest fighting raged. In this case, a column made up of NTC militiamen ready to go.

▲ A republican mobile column as it leaves Barcelona: a 'tiznao' opens the march.

▼ The 'tiznao' called 'El Caleyo' of the Popular Army of Asturias.

▲ Another image of the same vehicle, surrounded by Asturian militiamen.

▼ 'El Caleyo' with its crew.

▲ Armoured vehicle made by the Sociedad Anonima de Fibras Artificiales (SAFA).

▼ Republican armoured vehicle in Gijón, August 1936.

'Ebro', regardless of the manufacturer, but each manufacturer gave the vehicles their own design number, so there were several 'Ebro No. 1', 'Ebro No. 2', and so on. Used by the Republicans during the Civil War, the 'Ebros', built on large truck and bus chassis, were generally characterised by an armed turret, numerous loopholes to allow firing from inside with small arms, and chains placed to protect the tyres. The limited offensive capacity of these vehicles was compensated for by the strong psychological impact they had on the enemy with their noise, raising dust on the roads and their mere presence in the squares, which was fundamental in the first months of the war, during which the Republicans, ignorant of war tactics and lacking in command lines, faced a better-trained and more organised enemy. Twelve 'Ebro' were produced, each one different from the other; four of these were captured intact by the Nationalists during the fighting and reused against their former owners.

The Maquinista y Fundiciones Ebro built a series of at least four vehicles in August 1936. The first armoured vehicle produced by Bressel was the 'Ebro No. 1', which had a characteristic battering ram tip, which was used to break through any barrages found in its path; like all the others they were used to supply the advanced positions, set up in the first months of the war on the Aragon front, with provisions and ammunition. The 'Ebro No. 2' model was much larger, thus being able to carry more men on board, with an improved possibility of firing from the side loopholes. This vehicle was also used mainly for resupply functions, convoy protection, patrolling of communication routes and surveillance of the rear of moving troops. In contrast, the 'Ebro No. 3' truck sacrificed size and space to transport troops, favouring mobility characteristics, being smaller than its predecessors.

Other industries in Zaragoza joined in the production of similar vehicles.

Carde y Escoriaza of the Material Móvil y Construcciones factory, a heavy industry in Zaragoza, produced ammunition from the beginning of the conflict and armoured vehicles also came out of its production departments. The 'Ebro n°1' model from Carde y Escoriaza was designed almost like an armoured bus, so that it could offer a large load capacity for men and materials. "Ebro n°2" was an evolution of the previous one, on which a reflector was introduced and the shape of the mudguards changed. The 'Ebro n°2' took part in the Battle of Teruel, where it was hit by at least two bullets in the rear that pinned it down. For this reason it was the subject of many photographs, both of Republican and Nationalist soldiers, who had their portraits taken next to the vehicle. The 'Ebro n°3' model was very similar to the others made by Carde y Escoriaza, differing from its predecessors only in a modification of the mudguard.

MERCIER II ARMOURED CAR

It was built for the Nationalists in a single unit in Zaragoza at the Talleres Mercier factory on the chassis of another captured Republican 'tiznaos' that had been dismantled. Externally it was almost identical to the 'Ebro' armoured trucks, so much so that it was sometimes not identified as a different armoured vehicle. It was equipped with a turret, armed with a Hotchkiss light machine gun.

TORRAS ARMOURED TRUCKS

Another Catalan manufacturer of armoured vehicles of circumstance was the Torras Metallurgical Industry of Barcelona, which produced at least 6 different models, both with turrets and without, all characterised by extremely square shapes, which made them resemble boxes with wheels.

Among the armoured vehicles produced by Torras, the most famous is undoubtedly the Torras 2, nicknamed 'King Kong', the personal vehicle of the anarchist Buenaventura Durruti. The armoured vehicle was piloted by Antonio Bonilla, a trusted friend of the anarchist leader; 'King Kong' did not become part of the staff of the so-called 'Durruti' Column until some time after its formation. As the vehicle reserved for the transport of Commandant Durruti, 'King Kong' soon became the anarchists' armoured truck par excellence, becoming a symbol of the armed struggle of this movement.

GIRONA ARMOURED TRUCKS

They were produced in the Materiales de Ferrocarriles y Construcciones workshops, probably a total of 9 different models, between 1936 and 1937. The vehicles produced were all different, both in structure and armament, and, from the photographs found, had identifying marks and mottos that could be traced back to the CNT and the FAI. The 'Girona' fought in Durruti's anarchist phalanx, in the FAI's 'Los Aguiluchos' column and in García Oliver's 'Reds and Blacks'. The 'Girona 1', which had a fixed turret, was presented during an official ceremony in the Sant Jaume square in Barcelona on 29 August 1936, after it had been produced by the willing workers of the Girona Ironworks. These armoured vehicles fought practically until the end of the war, especially in the region of Aragon.

FERROL ARMOURED TRUCKS

After the uprisings that followed the electoral victory of the Popular Left Front in the February 1936 elections, in the coastal town of Ferrol in northern Galicia, the Regimento de Artillería de Costas No. 2 had at least four Hispano-Suiza buses converted into armoured vehicles, which were named Ferrol after the town. Unlike many other 'tiznao', the Ferrols were built before the war and were assembled by qualified military personnel and not by militia groups; although they had some aesthetic and construction differences between them, the vehicles were very similar. They had 6-8 mm steel armour, painted grey, and each vehicle had a number from 1 to 4 painted under the ventilation grilles; each vehicle was equipped with a revolving turret, inspired by that of the Rolls-Royce armoured car of the Great War, armed with a 7 mm Hotchkiss Model 1924 machine gun. On each side of the vehicle were seven slits for rifle fire and a further eight on either side of the turret. The front of the vehicle had two sets of ventilation grilles, installed to prevent the engine from overheating. Four examples of this large armoured car were certainly produced, but a prototype without turret was probably also built. On the sides was painted in red and black the crest of the Regiment de Artillería de Costas No. 2, consisting of a crab with a bomb and the motto '*Adelante, Viva España*'.
At the outbreak of the Civil War in July 1936, the Ferrols were the only armoured vehicles in Galicia available to Nationalist troops. They were first used on 20 July 1936 to transport ammunition and weapons from the coastal artillery barracks to the troops of Infantry Regiment No. 35 'Mérida'. Used both in combat and as escort vehicles in Galicia, the Ferrols proved to be very effective and efficient vehicles. Between the end of October and the beginning of November 1936, Ferrols were sent to several northern fronts: at least two (most probably numbers 3 and 4) in the Oviedo-Grado sector in Asturias, the other two in the La Robla-Matallana-La Vecilla sector on the Leon front. In February 1937, two Ferrols (most probably numbers 3 and 4) were in Oviedo, which was besieged by the Republicans, together with two Trubia tanks, placed in defence of the Campo de los Patos arms factory, facing about forty Republican armoured vehicles.
After the conclusion of the War in the North in October 1937, given the wide availability of Italian CV.33/35 and German Panzer I tanks, the Ferrols were deemed obsolete. Their fate is unknown, but it seems likely that they were still used for patrol and police duties for a while before being dismantled.

▲ 'Vulcano', armoured truck in Barcelona, following an armour-plating layout similar to that of the Bilbao armoured cars, although the vehicle was larger.

▼ As this photograph shows, at least two identical 'Vulcano' specimens were built.

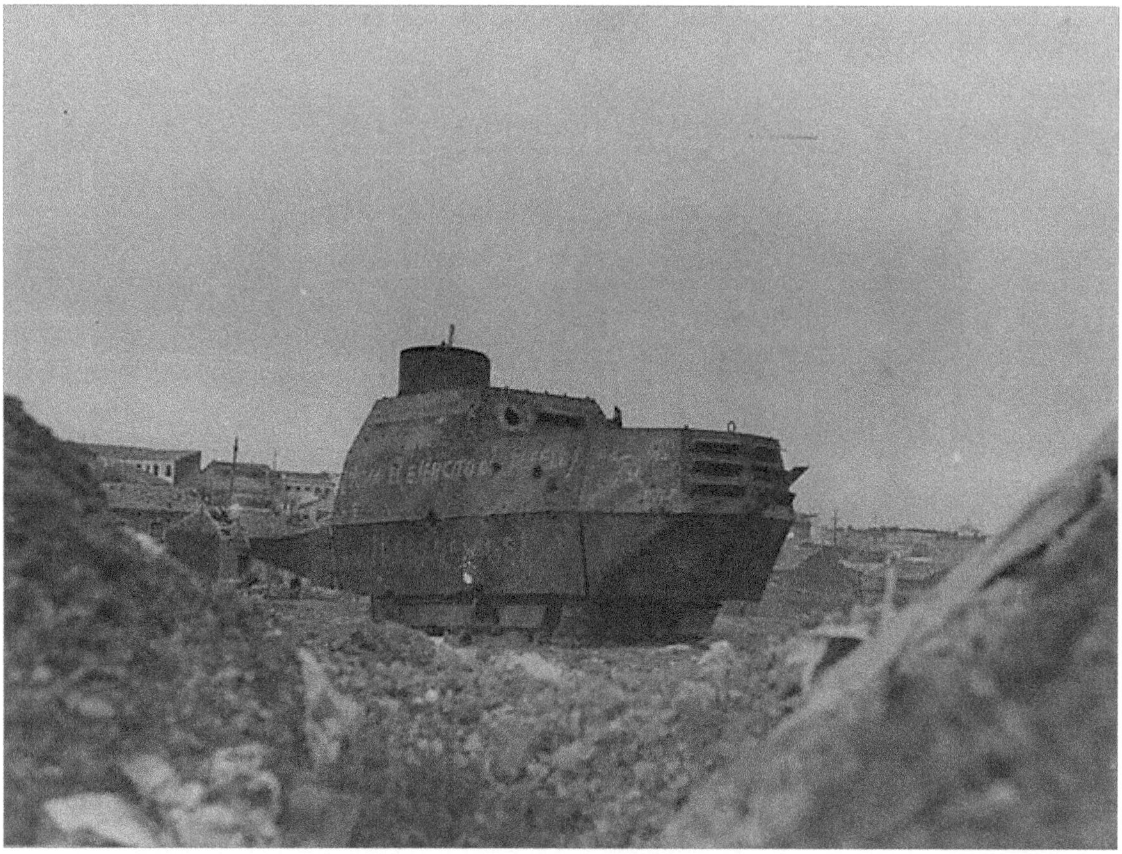

▲ A Caterpillar tractor, transformed into an improvised tank by Republican troops, destroyed on the Madrid front in 1936.

▼ Another republican 'tiznao' covered in grease, to facilitate the sliding of bullets over the armour.

COLOURING OF THE "TIZNAOS"

Even the camouflage colours and heraldry of the 'tiznaos' obviously did not follow any set rules. The most common colour, as we have seen, was grey (which, moreover, was the colour stipulated by Spanish Army regulations for armoured trucks[4]). Sometimes, using green, brown or sand paints, the vehicles received camouflage colours (without following any codified pattern), either in spots or stripes, or uniform monochrome liveries. Some 'tiznaos' were not even painted: examples with only rustproof paint are known, and others with no paint at all, with rust stains emerging.

The only 'emblems' on the 'tiznaos' were political slogans. Each political group or faction, in fact, took care to personalise their vehicle with the affixing of their own political acronyms:

- CNT - Confederacion Nacional de Trabajo (National Confederation of Labour)
- FAI - Federaciôn Anarquista Ibérica (Iberian Anarchist Federation)
- UGT - Unión General de Trabajadores (General Workers' Union)
- POUM - Partido Obrero de Unificacion Marxista (Workers' Party of Marxist Unification)
- PSOE - 'Uníos Hermanos Proletarios!' ('Union, Proletarian Brothers!')
- PARTIDO COMUNISTA (Communist Party)

and propagandist phrases such as '*Viva la República*', '*Arriba España*' ('Long live Spain!'), '*Abaix el fexismei*' ('Down with fascism') or the famous 'No *pasarán!*' ('They will not pass!'[5]).

▲ An armoured truck of the Republicans in a street of the small town of Santander is observed with curiosity by a group of boys... but also by some adults!

---

4 A circular of 10 February 1929, 'Real Orden Circular', stipulated that the Spanish Army's motor vehicles, classified as '*Autocamiones*', had to be entirely painted in a particular tone of grey, called 'artillery grey', and that the sides had to bear a rectangular wooden board 70 cm by 35 cm, painted in black, with an inscription, on two lines in white capital letters, showing on the first line the weapon to which it belonged (e.g. ARTILLERIA or SANIDAD MILITAR) and on the second the initials AMT (which indicated '*Automovil*') and the vehicle's registration number.

5 Famous and iconic motto coined by the famous Spanish communist leader Dolores Ibarruri on 19 July 1936 and later adopted by all republican movements as a symbol of the will not to yield to Francoist forces.

▲ The shape of the body armour of this truck used by the FAI - CNT is undoubtedly curious: one wonders what the actual effectiveness of this superstructure could have been. In the photo, taken in Alcoy, a second truck with equally imaginative armouring can be seen in the background.

▼ The armouring of this Hispano-Suiza van appears very elaborate and elegant. The vehicle was used by the Colonna de los Aguiluchos of the FAI, which was the last of the great Catalan anarcho-syndicalist columns.

▲ 'Tiznao' produced by the Almeria Railway Workshops.

▼ Another photo of the armoured vehicle of the Almeria Railway Workshops. The colouring would appear to be almost a uniform light colour, perhaps a sand.

▲ Satirical cartoon about 'tiznaos' appeared in the Nationalist press of the time.

▼ Interesting example of camouflage on a Spanish armoured truck in three or four colours, probably sand (background) brown and green (and white?). The sides bear an elaborate pictorial representation, probably in black, consisting of the inscription 'Tailler Mza Albacete Columna Internacional', the outline of a train and two clasping hands (the latter in white paint). The turret is armed with a Lewis machine gun.

▲ An unfortunately poor-quality photo showing the 'tiznao' named 'Navarro Number 5'; interestingly, bicycles are carried on the vehicle.

▼ 'Tiznao' captured by the Nationalists near a railway station. The new owners immediately wrote 'Viva Franco' on the sides.

▲ Republican soldiers climb aboard an armoured tractor during a firefight in order to reach the line of fire under cover of enemy fire.

▼ Detail of another armoured tractor, probably during the same fighting as the previous photo: it is impressive to see how crammed the men on board were, a condition that, in the event of an inauspicious outcome of an enemy attack, made the armoured vehicle a trap with no way out.

▲ The 'Tiznaos' often adopted truly imaginative and disturbing geometries, conceived by the inexperienced builders, with the aim of creating surfaces that could be more elusive to enemy blows.

▼ The so-called 'Communist' armoured car, so called because of the obvious inscription on the front shield. It was one of the best-known, but also one of the simplest constructions, built using folded sheet metal as protection.

▲ Picture of the armoured vehicle 'Escachamatas 2', at the end of its construction in the Maquinaria y Metalurgia Aragonesa factory.

▲ Two 'tiznaos' parked while a Republican mobile column was on the move: armoured trucks were used as escorts for the snake of vehicles in these circumstances.

▼ An armoured truck with a very square shape, photographed on the outskirts of Barcelona.

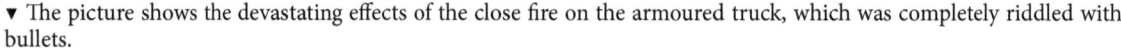

▲ A Girona 3 'tiznao', photographed in Barcelona on the parade ground of the 'Bakunin' barracks (which was called 'del Bruc' barracks before the outbreak of hostilities), where the Antifascist Militia Committee of Catalonia was housed.

▼ The picture shows the devastating effects of the close fire on the armoured truck, which was completely riddled with bullets.

▲ Extremely angular shapes, as improbable as they are, for this 'tiznao'.

▼ The crew of this armoured tractor is so heterogeneous that it almost looks more like a gang of Mexican outlaws than a group of militiamen.

▲ The same 'tiznao' as in the previous page: it was part of a series of armoured vehicles nicknamed 'Confederal' because of the conspicuous front lettering.

▲ Column of 'tiznao' in a city street. Interesting is the elaborate camouflage of the vehicle in the foreground, followed by at least two 'Ebro' armoured trucks.

▼ A stranded 'tiznao' is moved by a group of Republican militiamen. A stylised death symbol can be seen on the side shield.

▲ Photograph from a newspaper of the time showing the Torras Type 2 armoured vehicle, known as the 'King Kong' of the Durruti Column, which served as protection for Buenaventura Durruti himself.

▼ Another image of 'King Kong', unfortunately of poor quality.

▲ The history of this 'tiznao' is very curious. It was built using a truck used to transport potatoes to Buenavista de Valdavia, armoured by the Fabrica de Armas and used on the front between Aguillar and Baruello.

▼ Having survived the conflict, the truck was taken to Segovia, the armour plating was dismantled and the chassis was given a new lease of life... as a public service bus for the Sociedad Estación de Autobuses Palentino, until 1978, 40 years after the end of the Spanish Civil War!

▲ The prototype of Constructora Field's 'tiznao' Model 'No. 1' photographed in Barcelona's Plaza San Jaume, just outside the city hall, on 30 August 1936.

▲ One of the many armoured trucks built in Barcelona by Constructora Field for the Federacion Anarquista Iberica and the Unión General de Trabajadores, whose initials FAI - UGT stand out on the sides of the vehicle. From this model onwards, the vehicles featured a turret armed with a machine gun and steel plates to protect the tyres. Pictures of this 'tiznao' with the initials FAI - CNT are known. It is not clear whether this is the same model or a second vehicle, built identical to this one, since the camouflage (green serpentine stripes on a light background) would appear to be the same.

▼ This image, taken at the factory, provides a detailed view of the complex dark green striped camouflage adopted on the Constructora Field 'tiznaos'.

▲ The iconic and very prominent 'CONSTRUCTORA FIELD BARCELONA' lettering characterised all the vehicles built by this company from the Catalan capital.

▼ The most famous of the vehicles built in Barcelona is perhaps the Constructora Field 'N°9', as it is one of the most photographed vehicles and had the longest operational life, passing through almost three years of war unscathed.

▲ The 'Tiznao' Constructora Field Model 'No. 9' photographed during a break in the fighting. This vehicle is characterised by its uniform colouring, probably grey, and the inscriptions on the side 'ABAIX EL FEXISME!' ('Down with Fascism' in Catalan) and 'NO PASARÁN' ('They will not pass' in Spanish), as well as the number 9, which identifies the model.

▼ The Constructora Field Model 'N°9' taken from the other side, in a photograph taken in Caspe in March 1938. On this side are the slogans 'TERUEL SARA LA TUMBA' ('Teruel will be the grave' in Spanish) and 'VISCA LIVERTAT DEL POBLE' ('Long live the freedom of the people' in Catalan).

▲ For the protection of the wheels of the Model 'N°9', a sort of 'skirt' made of chains suspended from the lower part of the armour was provided.

▼ The 'tiznao' Constructora Field 'N°9' was captured by the Nationalists and put on display at the 'Exposición de material de guerra tomado al enemigo' in San Sebastian in 1938.

▲ The vehicles produced by Constructora Fields almost certainly include these examples with convex armour and turrets of a different shape to the Barcelona-based company's other vehicles.

▲ The rear of one of these armoured vehicles with convex armour.

▼ Armoured truck 'Ebro No. 1', photographed at the factory in Zaragoza in September 1937. The truck received a light-coloured background colour, possibly sand yellow, with grey or brown mottled camouflage.

▲Another photo, taken on Ramón Pignatelli Street in front of the Zaragoza bullring probably on the same occasion as the previous one, showing three trucks presumably all from the 'Ebro' series, on the left is in fact recognisable 'Ebro No. 2'.

▼ An operational image of the 'tiznao' called 'Ebro No. 3' on the Aragon front.

▲ Yet another 'Ebro' truck: compared to the vehicles seen previously, it features an extremely refined multi-coloured camouflage.

▼ A series of pictures of an 'Ebro No. 3' armoured truck during a military operation on the Alcubierre front in the Huesca (BNE) area.

▲ In this close-up one can see the inscription 'EBRO' inserted in a black rhombus, which characterised the vehicles produced in Zaragoza (BNE).

▼ 'Ebro No. 3' marching along a dirt road in the middle of the bush (BNE).

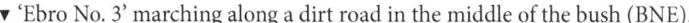

▲ Armoured 'Ebro No. 1' produced by Carde y Escoriaza.

▼ The same 'tiznao' seen from the front.

▲ 'Ebro No. 2' by Carde y Escoriaza: it is practically identical to the previous vehicle.

▲ Another 'tiznao' model built at Carde y Escoriaza, probably model 'No. 3'.

▼ The 'tiznao' named 'Mercier No. 2' photographed just off the assembly line. The resemblance to the 'Ebro' armoured trucks is evident.

▲ A 'tiznao' built by Torras Industries, the Type 3: this belonged to the Francisco Ascaso column and was one of the most representative of the 'workers' power' that was extremely responsive at the start of the war.

▼ Type 4 armoured truck built by Talleres Torras in Barcelona fresh off the assembly lines in October 1936.

▲ Rear view of two Torras Type 4, photographed in Barcelona.

▼ A beautiful photograph showing together, from left, a Girona 1 'tiznao', three Torras Type 3 and a Torras Type 1 displayed on the Rambla in Barcelona in July 1937 (Arxiu Històric del Poblenou).

▲ At right is Durruti's Torras Type 2, nicknamed 'King Kong'.

▼ Tucked away in a warehouse, probably at the end of the war, from the left are a Hispano Suiza 5, two Hispano Suiza 6s and a Torras Type 6.

▲ This armoured vehicle has often been confused with a Torras 2. In reality, it is a different vehicle, manufactured in the town of Olot (Gerona), which was presented in Barcelona on 11 September 1936 and immediately sent to the Aragon front, used by German-speaking volunteers (Mata).

▼ In the same photograph, Girona 1 (left) and Girona 2, in a square packed with crowds.

▲ Girona 3 with the initials of the anarchist Confederación Nacional de Trabajo in 1937.

▼ A series of Girona 5 armoured trucks photographed at the factory.

▲ Girona 6 armoured truck.

▼ Notice the very elaborate camouflage of this Girona 6, photographed in Barcelona.

▲ Ferrol No. 3 and 4 at the barracks of the Regimiento de Artillería de Costas No. 2.

▼ At the end of the civil war the surviving 'tiznaos' were sent for destruction by the Nationalists. In this picture the remains of a Constructora Field 'Nº5' and a Girona 5, demolished after the victory on the Aragon front in 1939.

▲ One of the prototypes of the Carro Ligero Trubia Serie A Modelo 1926 being assembled at the factory.

▼ The only known photo of the first prototype of the Carro Ligero Trubia Serie A Modelo 1926, photographed facing an obstacle consisting of a stone wall, at an unspecified place and date.

SPANISH-MADE PROTOTYPES

The Spanish Civil War was an opportunity, probably unrepeatable, for the Iberian country to put all the intellectual, technical and technological knowledge of its industry and its designers into the pursuit of a national armoured vehicle. In fact, the experience gained, especially in Morocco, had shown how important the tank weapon was in modern warfare and how important it was to have tanks and armoured vehicles up to the tasks required of armoured units. Spain in the 1930s was still far behind in the process of establishing armoured units and entrusted its units to a few decidedly obsolete means, as we have seen above. For this reason, there was a strong need for a nationally built tank that could form the backbone of the tank units.

The outbreak of the Civil War thus found a climate full of intellectual ferment, found numerous projects in progress, others almost finished, and aroused further interest in the search for a Spanish tank, which produced other projects, born precisely during the years of the terrible conflict.

CARRO LIGERO TRUBIA SERIE A MODELO 1926

The Trubia Series A light tank was the first tank designed and produced entirely in Spain, without foreign influence or collaboration. Commonly referred to as the Trubia A4, the first prototype was built in 1926, followed by an order for four more units, but these were only completed by 1934. The original idea was to produce 12 units, but the project was delayed first by the October 1934 coup d'état and then by the start of the civil war after the 1936 uprising. With this armoured vehicle, the Spanish army planned to replace the ageing Renault FT-17s, of French origin, that had operated for so long in Morocco during the War of the Rif. Unfortunately, due to the lack of funds available, the programme was slowed down and downsized, partly as a consequence of the convulsive political and social situation that Spain was experiencing in those years.

The first prototype was sent to the Escuela Central de Tiro in Carabanchel to undergo a series of tests, while the second prototype was completed in 1931 and the last in 1934. The first prototype in 1935 was sent back to the factory to undergo modernisation and repair damage sustained during the testing process, the other three examples were sent to the Regimiento de Infantería Milán No. 32 in Oviedo. At the outbreak of the Civil War, these three tanks were used by the Nationalist forces, while the prototype, which was still at the Trubia factory, entered service with the Republican army and was lost on 10 September 1936, during the Republican assault on Oviedo[1]. The three tanks of the Nationalist forces were mainly used statically to reinforce strategic points in the defence of the city. The first combat tank designed and built in Spain is not known to have been used in other combats outside the siege of Oviedo.

The special design feature of this armoured tank was the special turret, consisting of two overlapping halves that could operate independently, each armed with Hotchkiss machine guns; in addition, the vehicle's hull had slits that allowed the crew to fire small arms. Although it resembled the French FT-17, the tank was much more efficient in all respects, and was powered by a German four-cylinder 75 hp Daimler engine. Recently, thanks to the efforts (also financial) of Asturian entrepreneur Jorge Sandoval and his team, with which historian Artemio Mortera Pérez collaborated, a replica of this vehicle was built and is kept in the military museum of the Asturian town of Colloto.

---

[1] The Republicans also employed in Oviedo a Landesa tractor, converted into a combat tank, which was in the Asturian arms factory, together with the Trubia tank.

▲ Engine tests of an example of the Carro Ligero Trubia Serie A Modelo 1926.
▼ An off-road test phase of the Carro Ligero Trubia Serie A.

▲ The first example of the Trubia Serie A on the body of a truck, ready to be sent to Madrid after its completion. Posed in front of the truck are the workers who participated in its construction; on the far right is the factory's chief engineer, Rogelio Areces.

▼ One of the Trubia A 4 tanks used by the Nationalist defenders of the city of Oviedo as a fixed position.

▲ A Landesa tank, abandoned by the Republicans and immediately reused by the Nationalists, pulls one of the Trubia A4s used as a fixed defensive position.

▼ The spectacular reproduction of the Trubia A4, which is kept in the museum in Colloto.

CARRO DE COMBATE LIGERO PARA INFANTERÍA MODELO 1936

The Carro de Combate Ligero Para Infantería Modelo 1936, also known as the 'Trubia L.A. No. 1' remained in draft form; it is mentioned because it directly (and heavily) influenced the design and construction of the Trubia-Naval, the most heavily produced tank of the Second Spanish Republic. The main characteristics of the Carro de Combate Ligero Para Infantería Modelo 1936 were its small size, a two-member crew, an 80 HP engine, armament consisting of a 40 mm cannon and a mix of armour of different designs, ranging from 3 to 13 mm in two layers, supplemented by 25 mm cavities probably filled with wood.

"TRUBIA – NAVAL" TANK

The Trubia-Naval was a Spanish light tank built by the Sociedad Española de Construcciones Navales (SECN) located in Sestao, Basque Country, derived directly from the design of the Carro de Combate Ligero Para Infantería Modelo 1936. The tank was designed as an emergency when the Basque Autonomous State was created during the Spanish Civil War and decided to have its own armoured force. Given the difficult situation in which the Republican troops found themselves in the north of the country, almost completely lacking armoured vehicles, in August 1936, Captain Ignacio Cuartero Larrea was sent to Bilbao by the Trubia arms factory, to assess the possibility of producing armoured vehicles for the Asturian front; Cuartero Larrea had experience in tank design, as he had participated in the production of the Trubia Serie A. The new tank was armed with two machine guns, one in a rotating turret and the other in the front. The exact number of Trubia - Naval tanks produced is not known, sources vary from a minimum of 12 (more realistic figure), to a

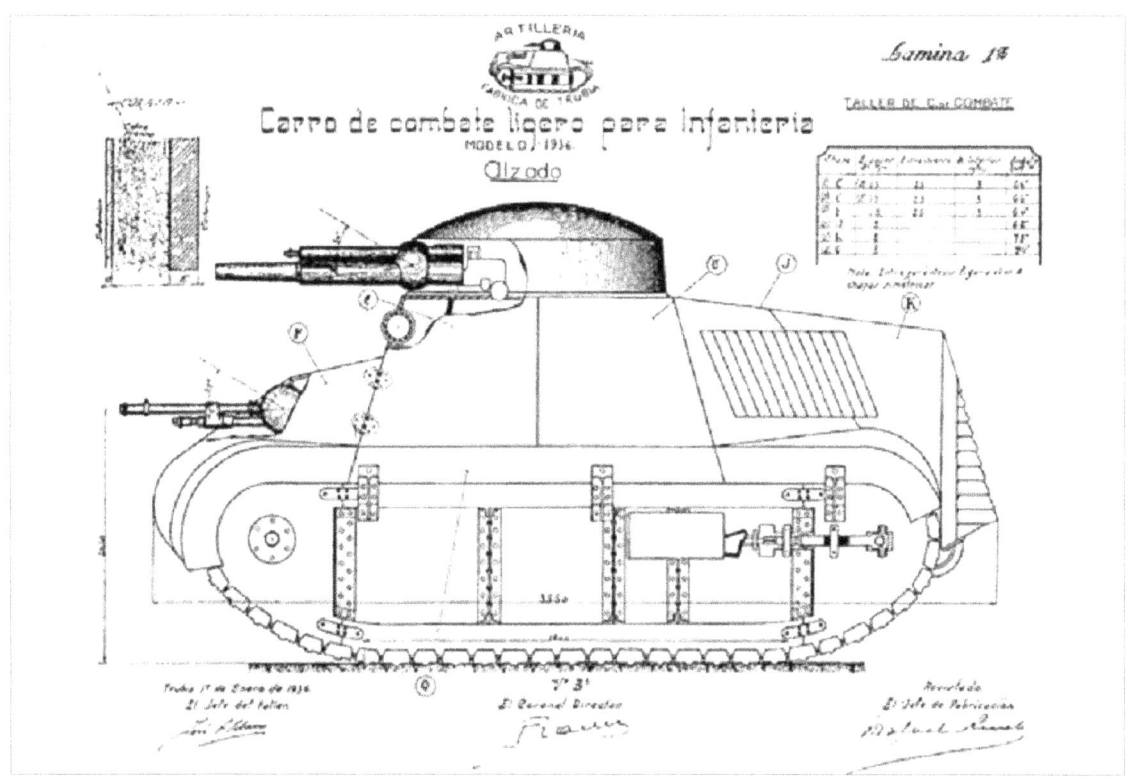

▲ Original design of the Carro de Combate Ligero Para Infantería Modelo 1936, designed by Victor Landesa Domenech and Rogelio Areces.

maximum of 45, which served in the ranks of the Republicans; some were captured and reused by the Nationalists[2]. Externally, the Trubia - Naval was practically identical to the Carro de Combate Ligero Para Infantería Modelo 1936, the armament was however different, as there was no 40 mm cannon available, which was thus replaced by a machine gun. The first example was equipped with two Lewis 7.7 mm machine guns, while the tanks produced later received two Degtyaryova Tankovy (DT) 7.62 mm machine guns each, a weapon that was also mounted on the Soviet BA-6 and FAI armoured cars. The secondary frontal machine gun was of limited use due to its location and the fact that it had to be operated by the driver, the crew being limited to just two men. The vehicle proved to be of minimal value in combat due to its excessively light armament, and was plagued by technical problems, in particular the rolling train, and characterised by a cramped interior.

The first Trubia-Navals probably came on line between January and February 1937: four were sent to Asturias to take part in the last major offensive and it is assumed that they were all destroyed. In June, as the city of Bilbao was about to fall, it was planned to move tank production to Trubia.

In March 1937, a Light Tank Battalion was created, which included five Trubia tanks in addition to some FT 17s and Russian armoured cars. On 5 April, one tank destroyed an improvised armoured car of the Nationalists and contributed to the capture of a hill occupied by the Condor Legion; later, the tanks covered the retreat to Bilbao. On 6 August the surviving tanks were incorporated into the Republican Army, as the entire Basque region had fallen, and were used to counter the Nationalist advance on Santander. At least one tank was captured by the Nationalists, who used it, unarmed, as a tractor.

Some sources (claim that the vehicle was named 'Tanque Euskadi' ('Basque Tank'), but although this hypothesis is fascinating and evocative, this name was never used during the Civil War.

▲ The prototype of the 'Trubia - Naval' tank: it is evident that the vehicle is directly inspired by the design of the Carro de Combate Ligero Para Infantería Modelo 1936.

---

2 The Nationalists showed little appreciation for the Trubia-Naval, as they considered them to be inferior to the armoured vehicles they had; those that were returned to service were most likely only used to tow artillery pieces, while the others were probably scrapped.

▲ The same prototype photographed on the other side.

▼ The conspicuous metal coat of arms applied to the sides of the Trubia - Naval. Specifically, this is the badge of the Trubia - Naval No. 12, which was captured by the Nationalists in April 1936. Although an agreement had been reached to recognise the involvement of both the Trubia arms factory and the S.E.C.N. in the design and construction of the vehicle, in the centre of the plaque we only find the initials of the S.E.C.N.; note on the sides the initials of the trade unions Unión General de Trabajadores (U.G.T.), Confederación Nacional del Trabajo (C.N.T.) and Solidaridad de los Trabajadores Vascos (S.T.V.).

▲ Basque Republican soldiers during a fight in Larrauri, north of Bilbao, supported by a Trubia-Naval tank.

▼ Republican soldiers photographed near a Trubia-Naval. The hatch of the tank is open and allows the pilot seated inside to be seen.

CARRO DE COMBATE DE INFANTERÍA TIPO 1937

The Model 1937 Infantry Combat Tank was a prototype designed in 1937 at the Naval Base 'La Naval' in Sestao for the Nationalist forces, studying the three main tanks involved in the civil war: the T-26, the Panzer I and the L3/35. The tank was armed with a 20 mm Breda machine gun and two 7.92 mm Hotchkiss light machine guns (one coaxial to the machine gun and one in front). In order to improve engine performance, the armour was reduced and, for this reason, despite the fact that the design was considered extremely good and the production of 30 units was planned, only the prototype was built.

Subsequently, this prototype was converted into an artillery tractor with the installation of a more powerful engine and underwent evaluation at the Escuela Central de Tiro de Carabanchel with good results, but it never reached the production stage and the prototype is still kept at the Academia de Infantería in Toledo.

▲ Carro de Combate de Infantería Tipo 1937CV Breda. It is evident how the vehicle is a kind of jigsaw puzzle between elements of the three main tanks involved in the civil war: the Russian T-26, the German Panzer I and the Italian L3/35.

▼ The design of this tank, which did not go beyond the prototype stage, envisaged an armament consisting of a 20 mm Breda machine gun and two 7.92 mm Hotchkiss light machine guns.

BARBASTRO TANK

The Barbastro tank remains an unsolved mystery in the panorama of tanks produced during the Spanish Civil War. It is known that only one example was made and that it arrived on the Aragon front where it took part in the fighting and was probably lost. No drawings, complete information or clear photographs of this armoured tank have been found, although some sources indicate that as many as three examples were produced.

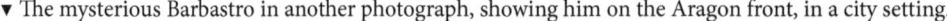

▲ Still shrouded in an aura of mystery, the Barbastro tank remains an impossible puzzle to solve, as only two poor quality images of this vehicle exist.

▼ The mysterious Barbastro in another photograph, showing him on the Aragon front, in a city setting.

IGC SADURNÍ DE NOYA TANK

The IGC Sadurní, also known as Sadurní tanks, were a series of armoured vehicles produced by the Benach workshops in Sant Sadurní d'Anoiaper , a well-known tractor manufacturer. When the Spanish Civil War broke out, the company was collectivised and the tracked tractors began to be modified as combat vehicles, in two variants: artillery and troop transport tractors and tanks, armed with Hotchkiss machine guns. The study of these vehicles was carried out by engineer Casanova and Joan Benach Olivella: Casanova designed the riveted steel shielding, while Benach Olivella took care of the mechanical part. Production and repair difficulties, poor armament and internal political conflicts in the Second Spanish Republic prevented the mass production of the Sadurní armoured vehicles. After the events of May 1937, their production was cancelled and the Cal Benach workshop devoted itself to repairing other vehicles (mainly T-26s).

The assault version (tank) was a model designed for frontline combat, but due to its lack of offensive power, it proved ineffective against armoured vehicles armed with cannon, such as the T-26B. For this reason, only two prototypes of this Catalan tank were produced in early 1937, which was effectively rejected by the Republican Armed Forces[3].

The artillery and troop transport tractor version had a lower, open and wider body that could carry up to six people. This version was more useful, as its reliability made it a good vehicle for towing artillery and transporting personnel, although it would never be engaged in direct combat against the enemy.

Nothing is known about the fate of these prototypes of either version: since the manufacturing factory was in the hands of the CNT union, it is likely that both were employed by anarchist units on the Aragon front, where the lack of armoured vehicles was dramatic. Breakdowns and lack of adequate logistics probably rendered them unusable in a short time, but there is evidence that one example was captured by Franco's forces in November 1938.

▲ The IGC Sadurní tanks were built on the same mechanics as the tractors of the same name built by the Benach workshops in Sant Sadurní d'Anoiaper.

---

3 It cannot be ruled out that these two tanks were converted to the tractor variant.

▲ Factory photograph of an armoured Sadurní.

▼ An eye-catching and aggressive image of an IGC Sadurní tank.

▲ A Sadurní in troop transport version of the C.N.T. union photographed in Barcelona in 1937.

▼ A 'Sadurní de Noya' tractor. Judging by the appearance of the occupants of the second truck, the photo must have been taken on the Catalan coast.

▲ Landesa artillery tractor.

LANDESA TANK

Shortly after the production of the Landesa artillery tractor[4], at the factory in Trubia, Asturias, work began on a combat version of the same, designed without a turret and with a single frontal machine gun, with similar suspension to the other tanks produced in Trubia. During the uprising in Asturias in 1934, two examples of this new tank were completed by modifying two artillery tractors, but the motorisation was plagued by problems that were not resolved before the outbreak of the Civil War, stopping mass production.

It is not known what happened to the two Landesa tanks[5] at the end of the uprising, but after the outbreak of the Civil War, they were put back into service by the workers and militiamen of the city of Trubia. The two Republican tanks were used for the first time in the offensive against Oviedo on 10 September 1936, in the course of which they were both stranded due to a breakdown. After they were recovered and sent back on line, one of the two was taken by the Nationalists: on 27 October, during a patrol through the outlying district of Naranco, a Nationalist Trubia tank captured a Landesa armed tractor, which had been abandoned on no man's land north of Oviedo, because it had broken down. The second Landesa tractor[6] was fielded by the Republicans during the last offensive against Oviedo on 21 February 1937, when, together with four T-26s, ten Renault FTs, and a number of Trubia Naval tanks, supported by a number of armoured trucks, they attempted to break through the enemy lines. The Nationalists opposed their Trubia A4s and the captured Lande-

---

[4] Commander Victor Landesa Domenech, an artillery officer assigned to the Trubia arms factory, and Rogelio Areces, the factory's chief engineer, who had already been involved in the design of the Trubia Serie A, embarked on a new project privately, based on an agricultural tractor, modifying it on the basis of the Trubia Serie A, but with some modifications, turning it into an artillery tractor, of which 10 were produced.

[5] There is no official name for this tank, just as Landesa Domenech or Areces do not seem to have given it a name. However, Artemio Mortera Pérez, one of the most authoritative scholars on the use of armoured vehicles in the Spanish Civil War, calls it 'Areces tank'. This would have a basis in reality, since Landesa Domenech joined the Nationalists, so it would be cacophonous to give the tanks, used by the Republicans, the name of an officer who fought with the enemy. However, no document of the period uses this designation; a document of the Servicio de Recuperación Nacional, drawn up after the fall of Santander, calls them 'Trubia-Landesa', probably because of their striking resemblance to Trubia-Naval tanks. Interestingly, the first edition of a booklet produced by the Republican authorities to teach soldiers and militiamen at the front how to read and write featured a modified Landesa tractor.

[6] Some texts report that there were more than one Landesa armoured tractor used in this attack, in agreement with the fact that a production of 15 to 18 is indicated, but these facts are not really borne out.

sa tractor, which had been put in moveable condition months earlier, worn out after a long period of service, in defensive positions guarding the main entrances to the city centre. The Nationalists' Landesa was still operational between the end of 1937 and the beginning of 1938, when, according to one testimony, it was seen on the hill of Santo Emiliano, halfway between Mieres and Langero, as part of an artillery unit, which presumably used it to tow cannons.

▲ A Landesa tank through the streets of Oviedo, during the battle that gripped the city.

▼ Image of the Landesa armoured tractor, captured after engine failure, by Nationalists defending Oviedo.

VERDEJA TANK

The Verdeja was a light tank designed at the very end of the Civil War, pursuing the dream of having a tank entirely designed and built in Spain, with better performance than the T-26. Designed by artillery captain Felix Verdeja, the tank vaguely resembled the Israeli Merkava, designed over 40 years later, and the construction concept was based on lessons learnt from the Civil War. It was a light vehicle, and priority in design was given to firepower, followed by mobility and protection. It was armed, like the T-26, with a Soviet 45mm cannon (although the design team had planned to equip the tank with heavier weapons, mainly 75mm short-barreled) and a pair of coaxial machine guns, which could even be raised in anti-aircraft mode, an extremely useful feature in urban or mountainous combat scenarios, which had so penalised armoured vehicles in Civil War fighting. The prototype was delivered on 10 January 1939 and remained the only armoured vehicle of this category built on the Iberian Peninsula. The crew consisted of three men, two of whom were housed in the truncated conical turret, to which they had access through a hatch at the rear. The canon's remarkable range in elevation, from -8 to +70 degrees, and its very low profile made the tank particularly interesting. The engine initially planned was to have a power output of 120 hp, but as nothing similar was found quickly, it was decided to use a commercially available 85 hp Ford, positioned to the right of the driver.

In 1940, a series of comparative tests were carried out between the Verdeja and a captured Soviet T-26B, which was found to be inferior to the Spanish tank. The latter was more compact, much lower and with a more elusive silhouette, and could pass more easily unnoticed than the bulky Soviet tank. It was decided that a batch of 100 would be produced, but equipped with a 120 hp Lincoln-Zephyr engine, but the impossibility of reaching a procurement agreement and numerous problems with the modernisation of industrial facilities meant that the project was abandoned in 1941.

Captain Verdeja did not give up and concentrated on devising an improved version of his own tank, named Verdeja II, with a more conventional configuration (engine and transmission at the rear and turret and combat chamber at the front), inspired by the experiences of the Second World War and with a hull influenced by Soviet tanks, but the project could not be developed quickly due to the same reasons that had led to the abandonment of production of the Verdeja I, together with the fact that the Government of Spain had decided to purchase 20 Panzer IV Ausf. H and 10 Sturmgeschütz III by the end of 1943. The construction of the prototype thus proceeded slowly and it was only ready in August 1944, but was not used. There was a brief revival of the Verdeja project in the 1950s, as there were no replacements for the T-26s still in service, but the arrival of American armoured vehicles meant that all interest in this tank was finally lost. The intact prototype of the Verdeja II was transferred to the Museo de Infantería at the Toledo Infantry Academy in 1973, where it still survives.

There are also design drawings for a heavier version of this tank, dated between 1940 and 1943, called Verdeja III, also created by artillery captain Felix Verdeja, which were not completed due to the difficulties in advancing the Verdeja II project.

The growing interest in self-propelled artillery developed in the 1940s and 1950s as a result of the events of the Second World War, prompted the Spanish Army to commission Major Verdeja to study a version of the Verdeja 1 armed with a 75mm L/40 rapid-fire howitzer, housed in an open casemate. An example was quickly produced, based on the existing prototype of the tank; this self-propelled vehicle was extensively tested, but, again, did not make it past the prototype stage, probably for the same reasons that had wrecked the Verdeja II project. Stored for many years in a state of neglect, after 1973 the self-propelled vehicle began a long pilgrimage between schools and barracks, to end its career at the Armoured Vehicle Museum at the El Goloso base.

▲ Captain Félix Verdeja, General Luis Orgaz Yoldi and Generalisimo Franco discuss the complexities of the Verdeja I tank project.

▼ In January 1939, the prototype of the Verdeja I underwent a gruelling marathon performance test at San Gregorio.

▲ Numerous tests conducted on the prototype of the tank designed by Captain Félix Verdeja demonstrated the excellent trench-crossing capabilities provided by the suspension and chassis.

▼ The Verdeja I breaks through a wall during tests at Carabanchel in May 1940.

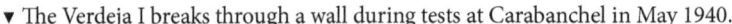

▲ The Verdeja I and a T-26B compared in May 1940. This photo highlights the extremely elusive silhouette of the Spanish-made aircraft.

▼ The prototype of the Verdeja II tank on display in the Infantry Academy Museum, Toledo. Note the more traditional configuration, compared to its predecessor, the Verdeja I.

▲ The self-propelled vehicle armed with a 75mm L/40 rapid-fire howitzer, based on the hull of the prototype of the Verdeja I to this day.

▼ Rear view showing the interior of the combat chamber of the self-propelled 75, which is kept at the Armoured Vehicle Museum in El Goloso, near Madrid.

UNL GOLIATH ARMOURED TRUCK

It was a large armoured truck, produced in 1937 by the Unión Naval del Levante company, probably in only two examples, according to the very scarce photographic documentation. In the Spanish Levante there were two large metal companies: the Altos Hornos de Sagunto and the Unión Naval de Levante company, which until then had worked for the navy. From 1937, controlled by the State, UNL was renamed Factory No. 22 and began the production of quality armoured vehicles, with the advice of Soviet technicians, following the models of the armoured vehicles that were serving in the Soviet army at the time (FA-I, BA-20 and BA-6). The Goliath was the last model produced by UNL, and we only heard about this vehicle in February 1938, when the factory was bombed and completely destroyed by the Italian Legionary Air Force, resulting in the loss of all technical information and plans for this armoured car. Today, we only know of the existence of these prototypes thanks to the accidental discovery of a few envelopes of photographs, which show the two vehicles, referred to on the pictures as 'Carros Goliath' and still identified as Goliath A and Goliath B, to distinguish them. The only known information can be deduced from the analysis of these few photographs. The two examples have obvious external differences, e.g. each has driving positions on different sides on the left and right (the chassis of a British truck was probably used for the Goliath A), slight differences in the turrets and in the front and rear profiles. The specimen with the driving position on the right (prototype A) has a compact nose similar to prototype B, but lacks engine access doors, the front fighting chamber is narrower and slightly inclined backwards, with the driver's seat slot on the right and machine gun installation slot on the right, and finally has a larger side access door than model B. The latter has a left-hand driver's position, a high, straight bonnet, a compact nose with side doors for access to the engine and the radiator protected by blind armour plates. At the front of the combat chamber, on the left side, there is a liftable slot for the driver and on the right side there is a slot for firing. The combat chamber is rectangular in shape and access appears to be provided by small doors, probably present on each side. The vehicles appear to be camouflaged in three colours, a green background and large brown and ochre stains. Nothing is known about their possible participation in battles, but at least the Goliath A appears to have been in the charge of a combatant department, as on the side is a coat of arms that places it with the 2nd Armoured Car Company of the 3rd Armoured Regiment.

OTEYZA MODEL 1935 ARMOURED TRUCK

Conceived in 1935 for the Guardia Civil, the Blindado Oteyza was built on the chassis of the 1935 GMC truck model T23 CS, had good armour and was armed with a Hotchkiss machine gun and a brandishing machine gun on the driver's right side. Although an excellent vehicle, with a better design than its contemporaries, it was never mass-produced.

ACKNOWLEDGEMENTS

The publication of my first research work was made possible thanks to two people, who believed in me and my modest literary skills. They are Luca Cristini of Soldiershop - Luca Cristini Editore, who gave me this opportunity, and Paolo Crippa, director of the "Witness To War" series, who introduced me to the world of military publishing, giving me precious information and ideas, useful to set up, start and finish the drafting of this first book, which will surely be affected by many flaws, due to inexperience. I must also thank him for granting me the use of photographs from his archive and some extrapolated plates from his book 'Italian Carristi in Spain 1936 - 1939', which also served as a basis for the drafting of the chapter on Italian Carristi military units, employed during the Civil War in the Iberian Peninsula.

My thanks also go to Antonio Tallillo, the talented author of numerous monographs on Italian tanks, who kindly provided me with numerous images that appear in this volume.

Finally, I apologise in advance for any errors, omissions, inaccuracies, particularly due to the unfamiliarity I have with writing for readers, this being my first editorial work.

The author

▲ Prototype of the armoured vehicle Oteyza No. 1 model 1935.

BIBLIOGRAPHY

Books
- Albert P.C., "Carros De Combats Y Véhiculas Blindados de la Guerra 1936-1939", Borras Ediciones, 1980.
- Ales Stefano, Viotti Andrea, "*Le uniformi e i distintivi del Corpo Truppe Volontarie Italiane in Spagna 1936-1939*", U.S.S.M.E., Roma, 2004.
- AA.VV., "*Storia dei mezzi corazzati*", Fratelli Fabbri Editore, Milano, 1976.
- Barlozzetti Ugo, Pirella Alberto, "*Mezzi dell'Esercito Italiano 1935 – 1945*", Editoriale Olimpia, Firenze, 1986.
- Benvenuti, Colonna "*Fronte Terra – Carri Armati Vol. 2/I*" – Edizioni Bizzarri.
- Benvenuti, Colonna "*Fronte Terra – Carri Armati Vol. 2/II*" – Edizioni Bizzarri.
- Barlozzetti Ugo, Pirella Alberto, "*Mezzi dell'Esercito Italiano 1935 – 1945*", Editoriale Olimpia, Firenze 1986.
- Battistelli Pier Paolo, Cappellano Filippo, "*Italian Light Tanks 1919 – 45*", "*New Vanguard*" n° 191, Osprey Publishing, Oxford (U.K.), 2012.
- Gianni Bianchi, Del Giudice Davide, "*Hombre sin medo - Uomo senza paura*", Associazione Culturale Sarasota, Massa, 2011.
- Capodarca Valido, "Immagini ed evoluzione del Corpo Automobilistico", volume I (18989 – 1939), Comando Trasporti e Materiali dell'Esercito, Roma, 1994.
- Cappellano Filippo, Pignato Nicola, "*Gli autoveicoli da combattimento dell'Esercito Italiano*", volume I, S.M.E. – Ufficio Storico, Roma, 2002.
- Ceva Lucio, Curami Andrea, "*La meccanizzazione dell'Esercito fino al 1943*", U.S.S.M.E., Roma, 1989.
- Chiappa Ernestino, "*C.T.V. – Il Corpo Truppe Volontarie italiano durante la Guerra Civile Spagnola 1936 – 1939*", E.M.I., Milano 2003.
- Crippa Paolo, "Carristi italiani in Spagna 1936 – 1939", Mattioli 1885, 2022.
- Falessi Cesare, Pafi Benedetto, "*Veicoli da combattimento dell'Esercito Italiano dal 1939 al 1945*", Intryama, Bologna, 1976.
- John F. Coverdale, "*I fascisti italiani alla guerra di Spagna*", Laterza, Roma - Bari, 1977.
- Mortera Perez Artemio, "*Los medios blindados en la guerra civil española: Teatro de operaciones del Norte 36/37*", AF Editores, Valladolid (E), 2007.
- Mortera Perez Artemio, "*Los medios blindados en la guerra civil española: Teatro de operaciones de Andalucía y Centro 36/39*", AF Editores, Valladolid (E), 2010.
- Mortera Perez Artemio, "*Los medios blindados en la guerra civil española: Teatro de operaciones de Levante, Aragón y Cataluña 36/39*", 1° volume, AF Editores, Valladolid (E), 2013.
- Mortera Perez Artemio, "*Los medios blindados en la guerra civil española: Teatro de operaciones de Levante, Aragón y Cataluña 36/39*", 2° volume, AF Editores, Valladolid (E), 2013.
- Parri Maurizio, "*Tracce di cingolo*", Associazione Nazionale Carristi d'Italia – Sezione di Verona, Verona, 2106.
- Petacco Arrigo, "*Viva la muerte! Mito e realtà della guerra civile spagnola 1936-1939*", Arnoldo Mondadori Editore, Milano, 2006.
- Pignato Nicola, "*Dalla Libia al Libano*", Editrice Scorpione, Taranto, 1989.
- Pignato Nicola, "*Motori!!! Le truppe corazzate italiane 1919 – 1994*", GMT, Trento, 1995.
- Pignato Nicola, "*Un secolo di autoblindate in Italia*", Mattioli 1885, Fidenza (PR), 2009.
- Puddu Mario, "*Carristi d'Italia in terra di Spagna*", Tipografia Artistica Nardini, Roma, 1965.

- Riccio Ralph, Pignato Nicola, "*Italian Truck-Mounted Artillery in action*", Squadron Signal Publications, Carrolton (U.S.A.), 2010.
- Rovighi Alberto, Stefani Filippo "*La partecipazione italiana alla guerra civile spagnola (1936 – 1939)*", Ufficio Storico Stato Maggiore dell'Esercito, Roma, 1992.
- Tallillo Antonio, Tallillo Andrea, Guglielmi Daniele "*Carro L3 – Carri veloci, carri leggeri, derivati*", G.M.T., Trento, 2004.
- Tallillo Antonio, Tallillo Andrea, Guglielmi Daniele, "*Carro FIAT 3000 – Sviluppo, tecnica, impieghi*", G.M.T., Trento, 2018.
- Tavoletti Francesco, "*Gli scudetti da braccio italiani 1930 – 1946*", Edizioni FT, Milano, 2000.
- Zaloga Steven, "*Spanish Civil War Tanks – The proving ground for Blitzkrieg*", Osprey Publishing, Oxford (U.K.), 2010.

Articles

- AA.VV., "*Estampa*" n° 484, anno X, Madrid, 1° maggio 1937,
- AA.VV., "*Italiani in Spagna*" in "*Prospettive*" n° 6, 2a edizione, Edizioni di Prospettive, Roma, 1938.
- Caretta Luigi, "*Hermanos no tirar – I mezzi blindati artigianali della Guerra Civile Spagnola*", in "Notiziario modellistico" n°3/14 – anno 32, Dicembre 2014, G.M.T., Trento.
- Cattarossi Emanuele, "*Carristi italiani in Spagna – L'occasione mancata*" in "*Quaderni*" n°1/2004, Società di Cultura e Storia Militare.
- Ceva Lucio, "*Ripensare Guadalajara*" in "Rivista Storica Italiana", Fascicolo II, 1992.
- Chionetti Bruno, "*Guerra Civile, blindati di circostanza e l'arte dell'autocostruzione*", in "Notiziario modellistico" n°3/14 – anno 32, Dicembre 2014, G.M.T., Trento.
- Dominique Renaud, "*Carro de combate ligero Verdeja n°1*", in "TNT" n° 43, maggio – giugno 2014.
- Yann Mahé, "*No Pasaràn, une guerre mécanisée improvisée*", in "Batailles et Blindés" n° 36, aprile – maggio 2010.
- Laurente Tirone "*Mad Max en Espagne! Les matérieles du camp républicaine*", in "TNT" n° 39, settembre – ottobre 2013.
- Manrique J.M., "*Algo más sobre los "carros italianos" en la Guerra de España (36 – 39)*" -1a parte in "*Historia Militar*", Maggio 2000.
- Manrique J.M., "*Algo más sobre los "carros italianos" en la Guerra de España (36 – 39)*" -2a parte in "*Historia Militar*", Luglio 2000.
- Manrique J.M., "*Algo más sobre los "carros italianos" en la Guerra de España (36 – 39)*" - 3a parte in "*Historia Militar*", Settembre 2000.
- Martinez Rafael Trevino, "*Armored lorries of the Spanish Civil War*".
- Montanari Mario, "*L'impegno italiano nella guerra di Spagna*" in "*Memorie storico – militari*", U.S.S.M.E., Roma, 1980.
- Tocci Patrizio, "*Le autoblindo Lancia 1ZM*" - 3a parte in "*Storia Militare*" n° 69, Luglio 1999.
- Tomasoni Matteo, Grassia Edoardo, De Renis Alice, Bottoni Gaia, "*Agredir Para Vencer – L'inno della Divisione Mista Frecce – Un documento inedito della Guerra Civile Spagnola*" in "Diacronie - Studi di Storia Contemporanea" n° 12/4 – 2012.

Other documents

- Colonnello Babini Valerio, "*Relazione sulle operazioni da Rudila (9 marzo) a Tortosa (19 aprile 1938*", Raggruppamento Carristi – Comando.

TITOLI GIÀ PUBBLICATI - TITLES ALREADY PUBLISHING

BOOKS TO COLLECT

www.ingramcontent.com/pod-product-compliance
Lightning Source LLC
LaVergne TN
LVHW072119060526
838201LV00068B/4924